W9-BXA-589

21st Century Junior Library

CARING

by Lucia Raatma

CHERRY LAKE PUBLISHING * ANN ARBOR, MICHIGAN

BOARD OF EDUCATION DIST. 25
ARLINGTON HEIGHTS, IL

CHERRY LAKE
Publishing

Published in the United States of America by Cherry Lake Publishing
Ann Arbor, Michigan
www.cherrylakepublishing.com

Reading Adviser: Cecilia Minden-Cupp, PhD, Literacy Consultant

Photo Credits: Cover and page 4, ©Jamie Wilson, used under license from Shutterstock, Inc.; cover and page 6, ©Maxim Slugin, used under license from Shutterstock, Inc.; cover and page 8, ©digitalskillet, used under license from Shutterstock, Inc.; cover and page 10, ©iofoto, used under license from Shutterstock, Inc.; page 12, ©Blend Images/Alamy; page 14, ©sonya etchison, used under license from Shutterstock, Inc.; page 16, ©Richard Levine/Alamy; page 18, ©Morgan Lane Photography, used under license from Shutterstock, Inc.; page 20, ©Monkey Business Images, used under license from Shutterstock, Inc.

Copyright ©2009 by Cherry Lake Publishing
All rights reserved. No part of this book may be reproduced or utilized in
any form or by any means without written permission from the publisher.

LIBRARY OF CONGRESS CATALOGING-IN-PUBLICATION DATA

Raatma, Lucia.
 Caring / by Lucia Raatma.
     p. cm.—(Character education)
 Includes index.
 ISBN-13: 978-1-60279-323-1
 ISBN-10: 1-60279-323-9
 1. Caring—Juvenile literature. I. Title. II. Series.
 BJ1475.R33 2009
 177'.7—dc22   2008032329

*Cherry Lake Publishing would like to acknowledge the work of
The Partnership for 21st Century Skills.
Please visit www.21stcenturyskills.org for more information.*

CONTENTS

Helping someone who is sick shows that you care.

What Is Caring?

"I'm sorry you don't feel well," Daniel said to his little sister Anna. He handed her a stuffed bear from her shelf.

"Would you like me to read to you before you go to sleep?" he asked.

"That would be nice," Anna said with a smile. "Thanks for caring about me."

Sometimes our actions can hurt someone's feelings. Caring people try hard not to hurt others.

When you are caring, you see what other people need. You take action to help them. You think about how your actions will help or hurt someone. A caring person chooses not to be selfish, mean, or hurtful.

Think!

Remember a time when someone was mean to you. How did his or her actions make you feel? Now remember a time when someone was kind to you. What did that person do for you? How did you feel then?

There are many ways to help others. This boy is helping his grandfather use a computer.

Be a Caring Person

There are many ways to show that you care at home. You can share your toys with your brothers and sisters. You can help them learn to play a new game.

You can also show your parents that you care. This means listening to them and helping with chores. Your parents do a lot for you. Saying "thank-you" shows them that you care.

Sometimes parents show they care by planning special meals.

A caring person chooses not to hurt other people's feelings. Maybe your mom cooks a dinner you do not like. You don't want to hurt her feelings. So you don't complain about it.

Is your little brother watching a movie you don't like? You choose not to make fun of it. Instead, you sit down and watch the movie with him.

What are some things you can do to welcome a
new classmate?

There are many ways to be caring at school. You can help a new student learn his way around school. You can save a friend a seat at lunchtime.

Caring people don't **bully** or tease others. Instead, they help friends stand up to bullies.

Create!

Talk with your family about caring. Make a list of kind things you can do. Maybe you can make a friend a birthday card. Or give your dad a hug when he looks sad. Then draw a picture of yourself showing someone that you care.

It is important to take care of your pets. Maybe you can help your neighbors care for their pets, too.

You can be caring in your neighborhood. Get to know the people who live around you. Take food to someone who is sick. Help a neighbor with grocery shopping or other chores. There are many ways to show you care.

You care for your pets by giving them food and water. Maybe you can help neighbors care for their pets, too.

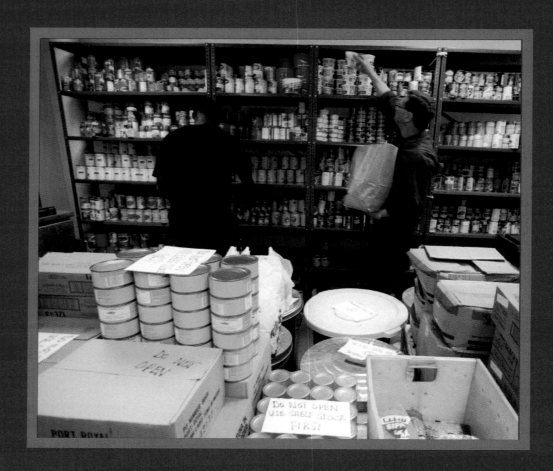

Volunteers at food pantries help collect food. It is given to people who can't afford to buy food.

Caring for Your World

There are probably many people in your community who are in need. Talk to your parents about how your family can help. You can even **volunteer** to help. Maybe you could donate food to a **food pantry**.

Recycling is an easy way to take care of Earth.

You can also choose to care for your **planet**. You can do this by **recycling** paper, bottles, cans, and other materials.

Why not plant flowers and bushes in your yard? They will provide food and **shelter** for insects and other animals. People will enjoy their beauty.

Look!

If you pay attention, you will see people helping others. Maybe members of your church are collecting clothes for poor people. You may see kids selling wrapping paper to raise money for their school. Keep your eyes open. You're sure to find many ways to lend a hand.

There are many ways to show you care. How will you care for someone today?